Blueprint For Success

Blueprint
For
Success
Live Life By Design

Ramona Rogers

Disclaimer

This book is designed to provide information and motivation to the reader. It is provided with the understanding that the author and/or publisher is not engaged to render any type of psychological, legal, or any other kind of professional advice. The content found within is the sole expression and opinion of its author.

No warranties or guarantees are expressed or implied by the author's and/or publisher's choice to include any of the content in this volume. Neither the publisher nor the author shall be liable for any physical, psychological, emotional, financial, or commercial damages, including, but not limited to special, incidental, consequential or other damages.

1st edition, August 2021

ISBN: 978-1-7365941-1-7

Printed in the United States of America

Dedication

I'd like to dedicate this book to my ancestors who stood strong in the midst of all the obstacles and challenges they faced. They made miracles happen despite the mediocrity of their times. Because of them, I and their future descendants have the opportunity to become GREAT and live a life that they always knew was possible. I am honored to be the manifestation of their hope and dreams.

Contents

Foreword

THE MOST POWERFUL ENTITIES THAT exist started with some kind of Blueprint. If you were to look up Blueprint in the dictionary or online, it would be defined (noun) as a design plan or other technical drawing or (verb) a draw up, a plan or model. We have already defined what a Blueprint is, so now we can actively identify how we can use one for ourselves.

The tallest, strongest, most impressive buildings, structures and homes started out as a Blueprint. You've seen them and been in awe of their foundation, attention to detail, and beauty. You've even driven by structures as they were going through the early processes. It is possible you saw land being cleared, huge machines being used, excavators digging and people walking about checking out what pieces or materials should go where. Maybe you can imagine seeing those things or imagine something being built. Blueprints entail learning hours, a target, and some knowledge of what the goal is. Drum roll; a Blueprint is simply a design, plan, or draft of something important and that something is you! If you want to create and sustain success, you absolutely need a Blueprint and I have complete confidence and conviction that Ramona Rogers will show you how to create and thrive with your own personal Blueprint.

Ramona has cracked the code on how to develop, implement and execute a Blueprint for success. She then decided she didn't just want it for herself. Through her expertise, testing, research, personal experience, and overcoming of obstacles, Ramona has done much of the work for you.

Earlier, you imagined land being cleared, excavators digging, and materials being put in the right place to start. You are at your starting point right now. When it comes to your Blueprint for success, Ramona has led by example and is giving away the secret sauce on how you can do the same.

Will this book help you?

The answer is simple. Do you want to be successful? Do you want to achieve success and sustain it through good times and more difficult times? Do you want to be a better version of yourself? If you answered yes, to any of those, I can assure you this book will help you.

Imagine knowing you are built for the greatest times and the toughest of storms physically, mentally, and emotionally. Understand that by reading this book you have prepared yourself with the proper Blueprint. Recognize that you are worth the words and knowledge you are about to digest, and it will prepare you and give you the confidence to be as admirable as the very buildings and structures you love to see as you drive to work through a major city. Your journey officially begins right now. You are now embarking on building the Burj Khalifa of yourself.

I trust my time, energy, and expertise with Ramona because I know she is committed and understands the value of a Blueprint and has created a system so others can develop and thrive with their own, too.

Sincerely yours,

Stan Pearson II, MBA

Introduction

For so many people, life a lot of times seems like a game that is not meant to win. I say that because there is such a GINORMOUS gap between the people that live life with all or most of their needs and wants versus people that do not. There are those who have education, resources, and money to live life the way they want. On the other hand, there are those who continually struggle just to make ends meet. Their life is filled with lack and never enough. The haves and the have nots are generally how these two groups are referred to.

I, for one, was a part of the have nots for many years. I remember thinking that a life of abundance was not attainable because that is what society dictated in the American culture since the beginning of its existence.

American history teaches us that there were a group of individuals that were able to build their wealth and prestige due to the many years of free labor from the slaves they owned. A nation of people were uprooted from their country and forced to come to America to do the manual labor of agriculture—working in the fields of farmers. The goods were the products of slave-labor plantations and included cotton, sugar, tobacco, molasses, and rum.

The key to slavery was to keep them illiterate.

Ignorance was the major control instrument. In order to maintain wealth, slave masters had to keep their labor force intact. Being uneducated, the slaves would never feel empowered to question their masters as to their rights to live life in this manner.

At the time of this writing, America is in an uproar over the continuous mistreatment and inequality of minorities. Systemic racism is a part of the American culture and people are fed up and tired of dealing with it so there are revolts around the world to address this egregious disregard of human life. (October 2020)

I mentioned this history because throughout my life's journey, I discovered that the reason the gap of haves and have nots exist is because it started centuries ago and throughout the years; there has not been a systematic way to change or reestablish how the have nots think and function.

That is until now. I have created a system to help future generations abandon their limiting mindset that has plagued too many for far too long.

I have learned one of the secrets the haves use to maintain their position in society.

There is always an ideology, a system, process, formula, or procedure that needs to be applied in order to be successful at anything in life. My system holds true to this philosophy as well and is called, Blueprint For Success, Live Life By Design.

This book addresses how Conscious and Subconscious thinking, as well as mindset, affects a person's self-image and outlook on life.

It also addresses the role that dreams and vision play in creating a Blueprint for success and living life by design. This book will offer information that will give readers the opportunity to make decisions that are based on the desired outcomes they want to see manifested in their life.

Book Timeline

I thought it would be important to mention the times in which this book is being written.

This is my second attempt at beginning this book. I began writing in October of 2020. The day I resumed my writing of this book was on November 12, 2020. The world is experiencing the Covid-19 health pandemic that has killed thousands of people since January of this year, with new case numbers increasing daily.

The United States has just held its Presidential election on November 3, (nine days ago) and the current President, Donald Trump, refuses to concede that he lost the election and has ordered his administration NOT to transition power over to the new President Elect, Joe Biden, and his administration. Disfunction at the highest level.

I mention this because under the Trump administration, America has become more divided than ever before due to President Trump's promotion of racism and white supremacy. Under his leadership, the United States saw the health pandemic affect the lives of so many due to his lack of response to the COVID-19 virus in its beginning stages. Of course, the have nots were greatly affected due to the lack of healthcare resources.

Millions are out of work. Social gatherings are almost a thing of the past. Schools have gone to virtual distance learning, and restaurants are limited in their capacity, so pick-up and delivery is the way they operate. Hope is fading for so many that life will be returning to normal. Economists predict it will take years to restore the economy. For college students, the college life is limited to no visitation rules being enforced for on-campus residential living. Athletic seasons are greatly altered if not all together canceled. Instruction from professors are solely virtual.

Some students even had to postpone their college education due to their parents being unemployed as a result of the pandemic.

The events I described above make the future seem uncertain for so many, but I believe that the information offered in this book will give a ray of hope that individuals can live a fulfilling life even after the pandemic is over.

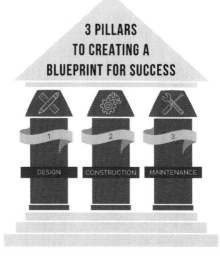

3 Pillars For Building A Life for Success Design, Construction, and Maintenance

A pillar is used as a support mechanism for building. It was the only viable choice to use to symbolize the importance of establishing a strong support mechanism and foundation in order to build a successful life. To illustrate The

Introduction

Blueprint For Success process, the theme of building a house will be used throughout this book.

Before a house is built, it goes through a lengthy process of being designed by an architect.

As a designer, an architect is hired by a client to produce detailed designs of a concept or idea that the client wants to bring to reality. Creative design ideas involve a great deal of technical knowledge and responsibility.

An architect maps out where things are going to be on the inside of the house. They provide all the specs and the inner workings to make the house function properly once completed.

Just like a house has its inner frame as the structure/foundation to hold the house together, each pillar in this Blueprint for Success process is used to be a support mechanism to build the life that an individual wants.

I've identified three essential pillars that should be used to support the individual that wants to build a successful life.

The three pillars are:

Design

Construction

Maintenance

In the pages to come. I will unfold the purpose of each pillar and describe the role each of them plays in building a life of success.

Invisible Elements

AN INDIVIDUAL HAS SO MANY aspects to them. Society has been groomed to measure people by their outward appearance. With this common ideology, the phrase, "You can't judge a book by its cover," holds true. Clothes and make-up have a way of camouflaging the true essence of people. Essence is the inner mechanics of character, thoughts, and behaviors of a person. That internal structure that makes an individual who they are. I prefer to use the phrase, Invisible Elements.

When I say, "Invisible Elements," I'm referring to the inner self that is the core of the person. Inner beauty, inner strength. Those intangible components of a person that can either enhance or detract from the physical outward appearance and representation. Anyone can say they are kind, but the actions of the individual demonstrate if the person truly is kind. These are the things that are essential to who you are and how you achieve, accomplish, and advance in life.

The definition of invisible is unable to be seen, not visible to the eye, concealed from sight or hidden. When talking about the inner essences of an individual, examples of Invisible Elements are hopes, dreams, gifts, talents, mindset, vision, and character traits. This is only a limited number of possible components that an individual may embody. I'm simply trying to paint a picture of the often-overlooked factor that confines so many due to the lack of knowledge of its importance and the ability to hone, nurture, and perfect these inner elements throughout the various stages of life.

To further demonstrate my point, here's another example. Air. Air is an invisible element that affects many aspects of life. A kite cannot fly unless the wind is blowing. A windmill's blades cannot rotate to produce energy without the air blowing. A boat with a sail cannot move across a body of water without air blowing into the sail which then pushes the boat across the water. Air is an invisible component, yet it is necessary and effective when in use.

The same holds true for an individual. The invisible elements are a vital part of how effective or ineffective an individual functions in any given situation or circumstance.

I added this component to the Design Pillar of my process because I wanted to bring awareness that even though it's vital to our existence, this is the piece of an individual that is not acknowledged, but it contributes tremendously to the core and growth of us all. Invisible elements should be strongly considered during the process of designing your Blueprint for success.

Chapter 1
Dreams/Vision

All our dreams can come true if we have the courage to pursue them.

~ WALT DISNEY

THIS CHAPTER IS TO CONVEY the importance and the power of your dreams. What better way to demonstrate this than by mentioning the greatest dreamer, in my opinion, of all times, Walt Disney. Walt Disney had a dream, and he never gave up on it. He encountered various trials being an innovator in many industries, and many of those experiences included failure. Walt Disney had a dream that he was bound to see come to fruition. In 1928, Walt Disney introduced Mickey Mouse in one of the first animated cartoons, Steamboat Willie. The rest is history. Walt Disney's theme of, if you can dream it, you can do it, combined with his unwavering work ethic, has encouraged many people over the years to follow their dreams.

From one cartoon featuring the animated character Mickey Mouse, Walt Disney built an entertainment and educational empire that has touched the lives of millions of people all around the world. His dream was that his projects would never be completed but would only continue to grow and change with the current times.

Another example is Martin Luther King Jr. In 1963, civil rights activist Martin Luther King Jr., gave his iconic speech "I Have A Dream." On August 28, 1963, some 100 years after President Abraham Lincoln signed the Emancipation

Proclamation freeing the slaves, a young man named Martin Luther King Jr. climbed the marble steps of the Lincoln Memorial in Washington, D.C. to describe his vision of America. More than 200,000 people—black and white—were in attendance to listen. They arrived by plane, by car, by bus, by train, and by foot. They went to Washington to demand equal rights for black people. And the dream that they heard on the steps of the Monument became the dream of a generation. (US Embassy and Consulate)

Unfortunately, at the time of this writing, fifty-seven years after that speech, Martin Luther King Jr.'s speech has still not become a reality in American society. His dream did, however, offer a visual representation of what the hope of a dream looked like.

Having dreams to follow is not something that is common or enforced by the masses in society. As a child you are told you can dream and become anything you want, but as an adult you are told to be realistic and that your dreams are not possible. In order for this toxic thought process to be eradicated, I offer the following acronym, an invisible element, to provide a new way to look at the importance of our dreams and how they should govern our decisions and actions.

D- Desire - A longing to acquire or achieve the supposedly unattainable. A burning internal feeling to accomplish the impossible. Having a strong intention or aim about your passion, hopes, vision, and goals.

R- Routines/Rituals - They keep you focused. You need to incorporate them daily to move toward your desired outcomes.

E- Emotions - They give you fuel for realizing your dream.

It's what ignites you. Emotion serves as the power for you to move in the direction of what you want to see come to fruition. Passion, hopes, and vision. Emotions dictate your decisions and actions and act as a gauge for the continuous journey down one path or redirecting your path somewhere else.

A- Accountability - You have an obligation to yourself to accept responsibility for your actions for doing whatever is necessary to make your dreams a reality.

M- Motivation - You must have a compelling reason as to why you want to achieve your dream. It will keep you focused during your journey.

M- Materialize - What is in your heart will make what is in your mind, become real.

S- Sacrifice - Be willing to give up your time and leisure activities to maintain a course of action that will afford you the opportunity to focus and pursue your dreams.

I know dreams is spelled with one M, but used two because these two elements are worthy of talking about to provide meaning and understanding of the many facets of life your dreams are tied to.

In the context of designing your life to achieve and accomplish, it's critical to understand the definition of the word dream. Dream simply means to consider as a possibility. You must dream big because it gives you something to go after. It gives you a reason to set goals to accomplish, in return you create the opportunity to live the life you want.

Dreams must be continuous. It's not a one-time thing. With each level of life, there should be a new dream to shoot for.

Here is the cycle for dreams:
- Dream
- Make Goals to Reach
- Create Action Steps to Reach Your Goals
- Goal Achievement
- Repeat the Cycle

Dreams are not supposed to be detailed. It's up to the individual to decide on the best course of action to take in order to arrive at the desired outcome.

Here are a few quotes by individuals who are well known for their diligence to make their dreams come true.

Albert Einstein says, "The person with big dreams is more powerful than one with all the facts."

Nelson Mandela says, "There is no passion to be found playing it small – in settling for a life that's less than the one you are capable of living."

Denzel Washington says, "Dreams without goals are just dreams."

I encourage you to DREAM BIG and then be willing to do everything you can in order for your dream to come true.

VISION

In order for anything to be accomplished in life, it always has to start with a dream or idea of what is to be. This concept is called Vision.

A Vision is the mental picture of the future you desire.

More than just a goal, a Vision is the embodiment of our hopes and dreams in a particular area; the picture of what has not yet happened, but what the future may hold.

Having a Vision about what you want to accomplish, acquire, or achieve in life is essential to have and it helps give you clarity of the end results being sought.

Without A Vision for your life, you waste a lot of valuable time going nowhere.

Without Vision you cannot put in place the goals and action steps that are required for your roadmap of your life's accomplishments.

In my experience, as well as that of so many others, the concept of Vision is difficult to conceptualize. Why is that? It basically boils down to knowledge, exposure, and experiences. Marginalized people, parents, teachers, and caregivers that have influence over students, tend to teach, and influence from their beliefs and point of reference of their upbringing and life experiences. How can you teach what you do not know or have not experienced? Vision is generally not a topic of discussion at the dinner table for the masses. Generation after generation, the same approach to life is like a movie you watch over and over again. Because you have seen it so many times before, you can predict how the movie ends.

My Vision is for the end of the movie to have a different outcome for the next generations that grace this earth with their presence. I envision a future where families and school systems acknowledge and incorporate personal Vision as the basis for building life outcomes. Keeping Vision at the center of everyday thoughts and life plans, will make learning environments and life experiences more meaningful. The importance of Vision should be emphasized so much that it becomes a part of your subconscious mind to where your thoughts and actions are habitually aligned with the Vision you have. As your knowledge, skills, and interest change, so should the Vision you have for your life. This has to be nurtured by teachers and parents so that the engagements in life continue to stay aligned during the various stages and seasons that life will bring.

I want you to understand that if you live your life without your Vision being the center of your thoughts and actions, chances are, the movie that you star in called "My Life," will end the same way as your ancestors. Life lived, but not fully experienced because there was not a destination envisioned to reach.

For those of you reading this book and thinking that you are either too young or too old to start living your life with your Vision being the driving force for why and how you function, I encourage you to ask yourself, do I want to live, or do I want to just exist?

Making the most of your life regardless of your age, was demonstrated by Helen Keller. She is a monumental figure in American history. Her tragic story of childhood blindness turned into a life of learning, breaking down social stigmas, and advocating for others with disabilities. Born in 1880, Helen contracted a mysterious illness that left her permanently deaf and blind at the age of two. Helen Keller became famous for overcoming adversity, and she accomplished a lot in a life that was both challenging and extraordinary. Despite her disabilities, she was determined to receive a higher education and enrolled in Radcliffe College. While there, she encountered prejudice from many of her fellow students who harbored the common belief that disabled individuals were of below-average intelligence. Helen was determined to fulfil the vision she had and graduated cum laude from Radcliffe College at age twenty-four.

Helen traveled across five continents to advocate for improved care and facilities for the blind and was awarded numerous service medals and honorary doctoral degrees in multiple countries. She is known for saying, *"The only thing worse than being blind is having sight but no vision."*

This quote means that your vision enriches your life and those around you. It makes your actions more purposeful.

How she lived her life with her blindness, ironically led to her giving vision to many others. She is a true example of what happens when you do not allow obstacles in life to keep you from having a Vision and serving a greater purpose. You should not only want sight, but you should also want a Vision for your life and be willing to see your Vision through.

Vision is a foundational element to guide your life and it benefits you in so many ways. It pinpoints the outcome you want.

Visions are driven by passion and dreams, and they are reflected through real efforts to create real results.

Without a clear Vision, you get stuck at life's crossroads. Having a Vision to reflect on helps you decide what direction to go in.

Think of your Vision like a destination. It is your end goal. It gives you a larger purpose to outline the little goals you set along the way. It is your finish line.
While pursuing your dreams, you will encounter some

roadblocks and setbacks. It is during these times that the Vision of what you want to accomplish act as a reminder of the desired end result. Your vision will help you stay committed and focused.

Vision simplifies life.

Vision should control your choices.

Vision should define your what to do.

Vision should dictate everything that you do.

Vision is about what you are here to create, and it should be so compelling that it pulls you toward it. That means your Vision should drive you to overcome the obstacles and opposition that you may face and provide energy for the work that has to be done to make your vision a reality.

Your compelling vision should include three things:
Your Purpose: What you are here to do.
Your Legacy: What you want to be remembered for.
Your Values: What will guide your journey.

Having these elements as a part of your Vision will help you be more productive in your daily endeavors and life experiences will be more meaningful because your thoughts and actions are centered around your Vision.

Having a Vision helps you to know what comes next. You must know where you are headed in order to live life at maximum capacity. Vision is a powerful motivator to help you be consistent and make sure your thoughts and actions are intentional toward your vision.

On *the other hand*, without a vision you wander aimlessly

from day to day, week to week, year to year with no clear direction. Without direction, you have no idea where your life's journey will lead you. Without vision, you get stuck in the perpetual whirlwinds and transitions of life circumstances. Life ends up feeling like *you are just passing time away*. No hope, joy, or aspiration. Without a vision, you could end up in the stress cycle where you experience more burnout and often feel as though your efforts are wasted and lack meaning. Not having a vision means you guess at what will happen next in life. You will stumble through life allowing circumstances, events, and other individuals to determine your destiny. This will force you to opt for mediocrity or the status quo of simply existing instead of living your best life. Not having a Vision causes you to miss your mark in life which becomes predictable because how can you hit a target that you never aim at?

A starting point toward crafting your life's Vision is to write it down. Keep in mind that crafting a Vision is not a once and done thing. It is a livable, moveable document. As you grow and learn, your interest, knowledge, passions, and priorities will change. Revise, reevaluate, and redo your Vision as often as needed.

Chapter 2
Conscious/Subconscious Thinking

"The reason man may become the master of his own destiny is because he has the power to influence his own subconscious mind."

~Napoleon Hill

Have you ever wondered why you speak, think, or act the way you do? For many, the way you think, and function is developed from your point of reference derived by caregivers and teachers that reared you. If that threshold is limited or low functioning, over the years the child that turns into an adult, has a low functioning mindset that yields a life of mediocrity.

This aspect of life plagues so many and is a key factor in the achievement and wealth gap in our society.

According to an article in the 2020 SAGE Publication, "Common Causes of the Achievement Gap," the playing field of life for minority- and economically-challenged students, is low, as it pertains to educational instruction and the lack of student success initiatives. This leads students to internalize their beliefs about having limited ability for opportunity and advancement.

I am a product of the public-school educational system. For many years, I felt inadequate and limited. The same system that crippled my mindset is still operating in the s same manner and failing the current students enrolled in institutions all over the snation.

There came a point in my life when I realized I needed to make some developmental changes about my life's possibilities. Who I was, my approach to decision making, and my daily actions. I went on a journey of discovery which forced me to retrain my brain to have an elevated Growth Mindset and vision for my life. When my mindset changed, my actions changed. When my actions changed, the results that I desired manifested.

It is my belief that if I can change, students that are growing up with the same lack that I experienced, can change their mindsets too if they are given the right information and understanding about mindset functionality. It will help them change their mindsets about themselves and their outlook of the possibilities of life. With this information, there is hope for a brighter future.

This chapter will serve as a guide to help with understanding thought processing and what needs to be done in order to retrain the brain to think differently about who you are and your ability to function and think at a higher level.

The two areas I want to address are subconscious and conscious thinking.

Designing a life Blueprint starts with an understanding of how our subconscious and conscious thought processes play a role in our daily behaviors.

Subconsciousness is the part of the mind that one is not fully aware of, but it influences a person's actions and feelings.

The subconscious mind is something that has a huge effect

on every action but is constantly overlooked. Your subconscious mind is like a huge memory bank. Its capacity is virtually unlimited. It permanently stores everything that ever happens to you.

The function of your subconscious mind is to store and retrieve data. Its job is to ensure that you respond exactly the way you are programmed. Your subconscious mind makes everything you say and do fit a pattern consistent with your self-concept. It is where all habits of thinking, and acting are stored. It has memorized all your comfort zones and it works to keep you in them. Your subconscious mind causes you to feel emotionally and physically uncomfortable whenever you attempt to do anything new or different. It goes against changing any of your established patterns of behavior.

Of what we do, 95 percent is subconscious (things we do that we do not think about; how people are programmed is how they are going to act).

To achieve success, 95 percent of your subconscious mind needs to be reprogrammed.

The conscious mind involves all the things that you are currently aware of and thinking about. It is somewhat akin to short-term memory and is limited in terms of capacity. Your awareness of yourself and the world around you are part of your consciousness.

The bottom line is that the habits and rituals that are inherited from family traditions can be detrimental to how individuals' function. Often, individuals speak, think, and act in accordance with what behaviors and mindset they have been exposed to. When behaviors and mindsets do not align with the desired outcomes, individuals must take inventory as to what their thought processing is and what must be changed to get to where they want to be.

The conscious mind functions very much like a binary computer, performing two functions: It accepts or rejects data in making choices and decisions. It can deal with only one thought at a time: positive or negative, "yes" or "no." Our single track minds can only entertain one idea at a time, so keeping it occupied with uplifting material has the power to block negative thoughts.

Brian Tracy wrote an article titled: "The Power of Your Subconscious Mind." In that article, he states that in order to grow and to get out of your comfort zone, you have to be willing to feel awkward and uncomfortable doing new things the first few times. If it is worth doing well, it's worth doing poorly until you get a feel for it, until you develop a new comfort zone at a new, higher level of competence.

Learning techniques to reprogram your subconscious mind will help you believe in yourself because your confidence will no longer be challenged by fear of the unknown. This is where you incorporate a new process or a new procedure or new system to get the new desired outcome. You must practice on a regular basis. But more importantly, doing so will train your brain to be in line with your true desires, hopes, and dreams for your life.

I'm a firm believer that: Knowledge is power! And Knowledge about yourself and how you function is Self-Empowerment.

This information is aimed to give you the understanding of how subconscious and conscious thinking affects your thoughts and behaviors. Now, it is up to you to use the information to make the necessary changes in your life that will afford you the opportunity to become the person you can become.

Chapter 3
Who Are You/Self-Image

"If you don't know who you truly are, you'll never know what you really want."

— ROY T. BENNETT

WHEN I FIRST STARTED ON my journey of discovery, it was exceedingly difficult to proceed because I had no idea who I was. Many days I recalled looking in the mirror and seeing a face but feeling a void from not knowing anything about myself. Building a positive self-image became my focus. I could not move forward without knowing who I was. In my search of self, I discovered Dr. Maxwell Maltz.

Maxwell Maltz was an American cosmetic surgeon and author of *Psycho-Cybernetics* (1960), which was a system of ideas that he claimed could improve one's self-image leading to a more successful and fulfilling life.

Maxwell Maltz's book introduced Maltz's views that people must have an accurate and positive view of themselves before setting goals; otherwise, they will get stuck in a continuing pattern of limiting beliefs. His ideas focused on visualizing one's goals and he believed that self-image was the cornerstone of all the changes that take place in a person. According to Maltz, if one's self-image is unhealthy or faulty — all a person's efforts will end in failure.

Maltz's information gave me a starting point for my journey of discovery. I even looked up the basic definition of self-image which in its most basic form, is an internalized mental picture/idea you have of yourself. It is how you think and feel about yourself based on your appearance, performance, and relationships that consistently impact your outlook on life as well as your level of happiness and fulfillment.

Maltz's teachings also revealed that self-image is a subconscious framework for how you see yourself and what you believe and think to be true. Every belief you have is a part of self-image. It is what you think is possible in life. He went on to say, the image that we have of ourselves controls our success and failures and impacts every area of life. We must change the self-image of ourselves that we have in our heads. The question then becomes, how do you do that?

I found it helpful to answer some basic questions about myself. Here is what I started with:
What are my strengths?
What are my weaknesses?
What are my gifts?
What are my talents?
What are some things I like or dislike?
What are my passions?
What are my attributes?

Answering these questions was exceedingly difficult because my point of reference was my past experience and knowledge which were minimal at best. My truth was a diluted version of who I wanted to become. At that point, I knew I had to establish new truths to get different outcomes. I needed to align my thoughts, behaviors, and actions with what I believed was my potential truth about who I wanted to be.

While this process may seem easy to implement into your

life, it was one of the most difficult things I had ever done. My will to change and my fight to stay in my comfort zone (subconscious thinking), made me want to retreat to the familiar. Familiar was my crutch because of the poor self-image that was embedded in me beginning at age four.

For years I thought I was incapable of being associated with anything that required thought processing or intelligence. During my journey of discovery, I finally recalled the deadly seed that was planted in my psyche which led to a form of self-imprisonment in the early stages of my life.

Death Sentence at Age Four

I remember the situation as if it were yesterday. When I was four years old, my mother took my twin brother and I on a routine visit to the doctor. During the visit, the doctor told my mother that because I was a twin, I would have below average intellect. I remember being called dumb repeatedly from the ages of four to eight. That doctor placed a death sentence on my life that day.

My thoughts and actions aligned with the negative words that were spoken to me repeatedly during my early childhood years. Those words shaped the negative image I had for myself for many years. The shackles and handcuffs of doubt, shame, low self-esteem, and the feeling of being inadequate, was how I lived my life. We all act consistent with who we believe we are. In my early years, I did not believe in myself, and I always felt like I was less than others.

The negative effects of my early years lasted well into my adulthood. But after studying Maxwell Maltz, I was relieved to learn that there was a way to change the self-image

I had of myself. This was a new beginning for me. I began to believe in myself and my potential to transform my life. I finally realized that someone else's opinion of me, did not have to be my reality. So I began to do the work to change my narrative.

According to Maxwell Maltz, visualization is a powerful way to help you change your self-image. In his book, Psycho-Cybernetics, he says that the brain has a hard time distinguishing between real and imaginary things and the brain does not know the difference between real events and imaginary ones that are non-emergent. He goes on to say that you have to practice what you want to become and that actions are the product of the imagination and habits are the results of imagination.

I've been practicing the imagination technique for many years. I attribute the technique to the person I have become, and the person I will be in future.

Even though I practice Maxwell Waltz imagination techniques to improve my self-image, over the years I've listened to numerous talks about self-image. One of my favorites is "The Invisible Force" by Dan Lok. Dan is an Author, Personal Development Coach and Motivational Speaker. Dan believes self-image in the physical sense, is who you see in the mirror. But we really see ourselves in our minds.

Lok says, the results in your life are the expressions of your inner self-image. People change things on the outside of themselves instead of changing what is on the inside of them (Examples: clothes, weight, hair color, jobs). Lok believes the strongest force in human personality is the need to remain consistent with how we see ourselves. The desire to elevate is met with resistance from the subconscious mind. The image that we have of ourselves controls our success and failures and impacts every area of life.

Lok believes that we self-sabotage ourselves in order to be elevated at a low level. Any form of elevation causes stress and discomfort and causes us to revert to the comfort zone of mediocrity.
In essence, we become prisoners of our own self-images.

The invisible elements that I'm sharing in the Design Pillar are an essential function of creating a blueprint for success. Keep reading to learn more about Invisible Elements that are vital to the Design Pillar of the process.

Chapter 4
Mindset Development

"The path to a growth Mindset is a [lifelong] journey not a proclamation."

- CAROL DWECK

SO FAR IN THE DESIGN Pillar I've talked about the invisible elements that are essential to the Blueprint process. All elements are essential overall; however, without being able to develop your mindset, the design process cannot be completed.

Over the years there has been a lot of debate as to what to do or how to develop a mindset that would yield a productive functioning successful person. Educational scholars and psychologist constantly study best practices for students to learn. In 2006, world-renowned Stanford University psychologist Carol Dweck's book, Mindset; The New Psychology of Success, was published. The book describes the science behind Growth Mindset and launched the Growth Mindset trend that is used in educational institutions and corporate settings all over the world.

Carol Dweck coined the terms fixed mindset and Growth Mindset to describe the underlying beliefs people have about learning and intelligence. When people believe they can get smarter, they understand that effort makes them stronger. Therefore, they put in extra time and effort, and that leads to higher achievement.

While on my journey of discovery, I learned about Carol Dweck and her Growth Mindset philosophy. The first thing that came to mind was, why wasn't this groundbreaking philosophy around when I was growing up?

It was like a pot of gold at the end of a rainbow. One of the missing pieces to my life puzzle. I now understood a concept that would help me develop my mind and thus achieve my goals and become the person I was longing to become.

During her years of research, Dweck discovered that the psychological trait of having a Growth Mindset, was the one thing that most successful people seem to have in common.

The Growth Mindset is the belief that Intelligence and skill can be developed through effort. In other words, basic human ability can be grown. This concept was not limited to a certain status of individuals. Its aim was to include the masses. Dweck felt it should be a basic human right to live in an environment that is overflowing with possibilities for everyone.

This is a refreshing position seeing as this ideology has not been the norm for so many for far too long. With the Growth Mindset being available to all that embraces it, the possibilities for life changing outcomes can become a reality. The playing field of achievement can then be level.

Here are some of the many benefits of having a Growth Mindset:
- Growth mindset people are much more resilient which allows them to overcome challenges and difficult situations
- Prioritizes learning over failure
- Are not afraid to take risks
- Prioritize growing over stagnation

- Believe they are always in a state of flex and transformation
- They don't attach their identity to results, instead they focus on the process of growing and learning
- Looks at challenges as a journey
- Accepts the long arduous path as a teacher allowing it to mold them into the person they need to be in order to achieve their desired results
- Understand that things take time, effort, and strategies to achieve

Dweck also studied the effects of the fixed mindset. In a fixed mindset, people believe their qualities are fixed traits and therefore cannot change. These people document their intelligence and talents rather than working to develop and improve them. They also believe that talent alone leads to success, and effort is not required. Unfortunately, the educational system has crippled a great deal of its students over decades due to the systematic approach to fostering a Fixed Mindset outlook on life. This mindset is all too common.

Here are some additional downsides of having a Fixed Mindset:

- People believe you were born with it or you were not and you cannot change
- Fixed Mindsets don't want to challenge themselves because they believe intelligence is fixed
- They look at failure as a results of who they are as a person
- Lack of knowledge is an indicator of stupidity and failure once, to them, means failure always
- Thinks that learning should be effortless
- Avoids mistakes at all cost

- Views challenges as roadblocks and barriers
- Limits what success is and who can achieve it

The outcomes of a Fixed Mindset lead to a life of lack and mediocrity. On the other hand, adopting a Growth Mindset will allow you to develop yourself and achieve all that you put your mind, heart, and hands to do.

There is a process, formula, or procedure to everything. That is something I wish I would have learned growing up. I was educated to have a Fixed Mindset; therefore, understanding that in order to learn a new concept or skill, you have to have a method or system for the learning process to take place. The same holds true for developing a Growth Mindset. Here are three things that have to be implemented in order to start fostering a Growth Mindset.

Three Steps To Develop A Growth Mindset

1. Understand that it exists and that it is possible for the brain to change. (Neuro-science has learned that our minds are not fixed.)

2. Focus on process over results. People need to internalize that they can change their results by changing their process.

Need to know how to:
- Create a process
- Alter or change it
- Produce results from it

This is a process of creating and defining it until you reach your desired results. The results are measured and paid attention to only as an indicator of how well the process works.
3. You must do challenging things to have a chance at foster-

ing the Growth Mindset. You must step out of your comfort zone. People who do not leave their comfort zone believe that their success is due to innate talent. Never being challenged gives them a false sense of reality. Going outside of your comfort zone forces you to adapt the Growth Mindset to avoid breaking under the weight of adversity. You must focus on and adjust your process because you can't possibly achieve the results desired with your current one.

This book and the processes that are included are results of me developing a Growth Mindset. Getting out of my comfort zone helped me build my confidence to go after the things I wanted in life and reach my goals despite the challenges and obstacles that presented themselves along the way. All obstacles are meant to elevate your mindset, build your confidence, which in turn places you one step closer to realizing your goal or fulfilling a dream.

THE INTERNAL STRUCTURE

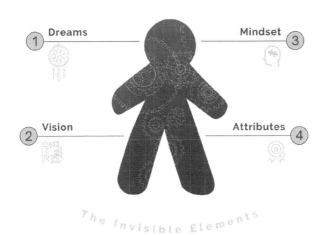

Chapter 5
The Great Change Process

"Change is inevitable. Growth is optional."

— John C. Maxwell

So far, I've talked about the elements that make up the Design Pillar of my Blueprint For Success process. These elements target the internal, foundational aspect of an individual.

You have made it to this portion of the book so you have been exposed to what can help you move forward to start the designing process to build yourself internally.

I am a firm believer in the concept of breaking away from the norms that keep you surrounded by struggle and mediocrity. I subscribe to the philosophy of, "When you know better, you do better." Changing the norm is a necessary yet difficult process. Individuals need to accept and learn how to view changes in life as layers of growth that help make up a productive, well-rounded person. With the understanding that change is a practiced process, individuals can limit stress, anxiety, and discomfort when the swift winds of change blow.

At some point an individual must decide as to whether they are willing to invest the energy and effort into living life by design or to continue to live life as it comes.

As mentioned numerous times before throughout this book, there is a process or procedure to just about everything in life. Once I learned that concept, my purpose became to create processes and systems that would help others achieve and succeed in life. It is my belief that all humans have the capacity to be great. And that's a process as well that I demonstrate in my book GR8NESS In The Making. That process is a formula and is the maintenance pillar of Blueprint For Success. (We will discuss that in a later chapter.)

Change is inevitable. It is going to happen in every aspect of life. In this instance, you can control the outcomes of the changes that will happen. Effective implementation of systems, thoughts, and habits that will yield to desired outcomes, is the key if you really want to live your life by design.

If anyone desires to be great or to live the life that they want, they will have to go through a process of change. I believe that there is a Change Process that must be identified and followed in order to realize how or why the arrival at a desired outcome is possible. There must be a way to connect the dots.

Keeping with the building theme, the building blocks that I have identified to help with the element of change is what I refer to as, "The Great Change Process."

The GREAT CHANGE PROCESS consists of Five Components:

Awareness
New Information
Mindset Shift
Decision
Outcomes or Desired Results

Awareness simply means being made aware of something. In this case, it would be the fact that you aren't living life the way you want or experiencing the results you want. Acknowledging that there is a problem or issue is the first thing that must be addressed. The question then becomes, what has to be done in order to arrive at the desired outcome?

This is where new information, knowledge, and education come in. It doesn't matter how you acquire the new information, knowledge, or education, all avenues are about learning skills and inputting new knowledge and understanding.

James Mangan, Author of, You Can Do Anything, says this: "Knowledge is knowledge only when it takes a shape, when it can be put into words, or reduced to a principle — and it's now up to you to go to work on your own gold mine, to refine the crude ore."

With new knowledge and understanding, behaviors should change, but it is totally up to the individual.

New information should bring about a new mindset. I talked about mindset development in a previous chapter. This is a time to recognize and apply the Growth Mindset model. Remember, the Growth Mindset is the belief that intelligence and skill can be developed through effort. In other words, basic human ability can be grown. The Great Change Process helps identify when implementation is necessary.

So let us recap what we have learned so far about the Great Change Process. First there must be an awareness that there is a problem. This should cause curiosity to seek new information and education, which is the second element. New information and education provide access and opportunity for an enhanced life.

The third element is mindset shift. Understanding that the potential to get better at anything is a possibility, takes away pressure and anxiety, allowing growth to be self-paced, but possible to all.

Once you get past awareness, information, and mindset shift, the fourth element is decision. You still must decide if you want to make the necessary changes in your approach to life. There must be a decision of how you want to move forward. Whatever you decide, you will arrive at an outcome. A planned desired outcome would be ideal; however; the individual has to choose.

Awareness causes curiosity.

Curiosity forces you to seek new information and education. New information and education allows you to maneuver better in life and it should elevate your mindset. A new mindset should bring about better decision making. Better decision making brings new behavior patterns. New behavior patterns should bring about desired outcomes.

Once you make the decision that you want your outcomes in life to change, your internal fight should force you to do all the things necessary to make it happen.

Change is a necessary component for life. Embrace it and use the process to design your life.

Awareness
New Information
Mindset Shift
Decision
Outcomes

THE GREAT CHANGE PROCESS

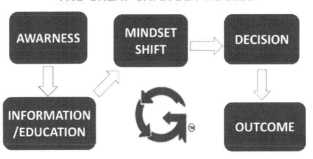

Congratulations, you have just read about the Design Pillar of The Blueprint for Success, Live Life by Design process.

Because it contains a number of change elements, I would suggest that you read about this pillar several times to get a better understanding of its components.

The design process is not a one-time excursion, but a lifetime commitment to self. Becoming the best version of yourself on a consistent basis will require you to implement the elements from the Design Pillar into every aspect of life and during every season of life.

The second pillar of The Blueprint for Success process is the construction pillar.

Construction means the process that consists of building or assembling a building or infrastructure. For the sake of mental imagery and to grasp the concept of an individual constructing their life, I again will reference construction of a house to the construction of building a successful life.

When a house is ready to be constructed, the builder makes a schedule for all subcontractors that have their specific craft or expertise to complete, for the house to be constructed in a timely manner. The internal tasks must be done prior to external tasks, so scheduling the subcontractors sequentially is crucial. Every piece of wire, wood, nail, concrete, or brick plays a part in the overall functionality and beautification of the house. All materials are harmoniously constructed to create a home for its residents.

This book, and the process that is detailed on its pages, can be viewed in the same manner. You, the contractor, have the desire to build a successful life. For the purpose of this book and this process, in order to construct a successful life, I am going to focus on the elements of goals and systems for the construction pillar.

Goals and systems are vital to The Blueprint For Success process. These components, when practiced and mastered, will lead one to achieve the results and outcomes that are desired. Intentional activity toward the desired outcome is key.

While researching for this book, I found that there has been much debate as to which one is better, goals or systems?

Over the years, personal development coaches such as Earl Nightingale and Brian Tracy have led people to accomplish and achieve great things in life by stressing the importance of goal setting. Now there is a new age thought that says setting goals is not necessary. Creating systems to achieve and advance should be done instead. Author Scott Adams expresses this in his book, How To Fail At Almost Everything And Still Win Big!

I don't believe one can survive without the other. The elements must coexist in order to build a successful life for the individual. Most goals are not achievable without systems, and systems cannot be evaluated without comparing them to the goal they are intended to serve.

Chapter 6
Goals

"Setting goals is the first step in turning the invisible into the visible"

- TONY ROBBINS

GOALS ARE VITAL TO THE Blueprint For Success process. These components, when practiced and mastered, will lead you to achieve the results and outcomes that are desired. Intentional activity toward the desired outcome is key.

This chapter will give you some insight on how to use goals to construct/build the successful life you want.

We must first begin with goals. Goals are the targets toward which you point your life. Goals give you a starting point and a destination to reach. Goals give you focus and help measure progress. Writing goals down helps you to see where you are going, what changes you need to make, and if you are progressing toward your desired result.

Goals Help You Determine What You Want in Life.

When setting goals, I encourage others to set SMART goals. SMART is just an acronym for a goal to be:

S- Specific

M-Measurable

A-Attainable

R-Realistic

T-Timely

Specific. The goal should have a clear, highly specific endpoint. If your goal is too vague, it will not be SMART.

Measurable. You need to be able to accurately track your progress, so you can judge when a goal will be met. How will you measure your progress?

Here are a few tools that can be utilized to measure progress:

- Facts and figures
- Checklists
- Task and timelines
- Record progress and problems

Attainable. Setting a goal that is too ambitious will cause you to struggle to achieve it. This will cause undue stress and derail your motivation for completing your goal. Set goals that are realistic. Progress is the key.

Relevant. The goal you pick should be pertinent to the desired outcome. Make sure goals are closely connected to what you want to achieve.

Timely. Set a timeframe for your goal. It helps keep you focused and on track.

Applying the SMART approach to Short-Term and Long-Term goals for every area of your life will assist you with setting goals that can be reached by actively pursuing your goals daily and taking the necessary actions that will help the goal become reality. Short-Term goals should be set for thirty days, sixty days, ninety days, one year, and two years. Long-Term goals should be set for five years, and ten years.

The concept of goal setting is not a new phenomenon. Goal setting is talked about, yet people have not practiced it enough to make goal setting a habit. They still ask the question, what is the point? The whole point is that you envision a better future for yourself. And, like the theme of this book of building you, the same holds true for building toward your future. It is done through goal setting.

Some aspects of life call for your actions to be intentional. Goal setting serves your life in that way by allowing you to plan where you want to go and then devising a plan of action steps that will get you there. The key to goal setting is that they need to be challenging. Your goals should stretch you out of your comfort zone. That is the only way you will grow.

Speaking of challenging goals, I'd like to share with you how I applied the SMART goal approach to losing weight.

Most people would agree that losing weight is one of the hardest things to do. Every fiber of your being is challenged. It requires commitment, planning, and discipline. Here is how I used the SMART goal method when I wanted to lose weight. I had blossomed, to put it nicely, to almost 200 pounds, (I'm only five foot three inches so that was not a good look for me needless to say!) I could not fit in any clothes in my closet except the items that were made of material that stretched. I had a compelling enough reason to set the goal and to see it through.

Specific

I planned to lose thirty pounds in six months by eating healthy, walking four to six miles five times per week, lifting weights three times per week, and drinking at least 64 ounces of water per day.

Measurable

Weigh myself every Monday morning to check my progress and document on a calendar. Try on clothes that I want to fit back in and take pictures once a month so show my progress.

Attainable

Losing thirty pounds in six months equated to five pounds per month. Losing 1.5 pounds per week is attainable.

Relevant

I had a closet full of clothes that I could not fit. It was more beneficial financially and from a health perspective to lose the weight so I could feel better and not spend a lot of money on new clothes.

Timely

I set my goal to be completed in a six-month timeframe which was realistic. My timeline allowed for any setbacks that can occur when setting a goal to lose weight.

Accomplishing my goal not only boosted my confidence, but my commitment to my goal also encouraged others to set their own SMART approach to reach their weight loss goal.

Personal development coach, Tony Robbins says, "Setting progressive goals that allow small wins helps you move on to larger achievements. These small goals lead to progress, which is the only thing you really need to feel fulfilled and happy." Tony also says, "Without a clear target, you'll never hit your mark. That's why it's crucial to learn how to set goals that are clear, measurable and actionable."

Most famous people are famous because they followed their goals and put in the work to bring their goals into fruition. The same holds true for many people who are not in the spotlight. Common everyday people have found ways to reach their goals. Before writing this book, I conducted a focus group and asked the question, how has goal setting impacted your life?

Here are a few of their responses:

"Goal setting has always proven to be my motivation for accomplishing things in life. Fail to plan, plan to fail. Internally a benefit for me has been gaining a concentrated focus in my tasks. Knowing what I had to do and how to get it done provided direction and motivation to get things done."

~ Jamal West
Entrepreneur

"Goal setting has always been more abstract for me... never written down or verbalized ... I just know what I want and start working towards it ... as a result, visualization was a must ... I had to see in my mind what it would take."

~ Charles Marshall
Retired United States Navy Commander
US Government Civil Servant
Entrepreneur

"Goal setting is definitely key to success. It's impacted my life by giving me clear direction and a path forward. It's also made me accountable to myself for reaching my goals and goals make you take ownership of your future and success and not rely on someone else. Goals put responsibility squarely on the individual where it should be."

- Ramon Watkins
Corporate Attorney

As you can see by the quotes given, the decision to be the master of your own fate is personal and empowering. These individuals set their sights on where they wanted to end up and then did everything they could to ensure they would arrive at their desired destination.

Goal setting will aid you in constructing many facets of life. Stay diligent in your pursuit and always be willing to pause and evaluate whether the goal you are pursuing, and action steps being implemented, are a good fit for the goal you are trying to achieve.

Constructing a successful life is not an easy undertaking, but it is possible. Keeping with our house construction theme, goals can be viewed as bricks to build your life. Individually, bricks are small rectangular shaped objects made of clay. Collectively, bricks provide stability for the home's exterior. The same concept can apply to the goal setting and system creating process each time a goal is reached. That means something has been accomplished or achieved. These events on your journey signify the bricks that are going to be a part of your finished constructed life of success. In essence, you are building yourself and your future at the same time.

After reading this chapter, I'm sure you may be wondering: if goal setting is so important, then why is it so difficult?

There are an array of reasons why people find goal setting difficult. Here are the most common ones:

You do not like the process or the work that is required to reach your desired outcomes.

Setting goals that do not require much effort, which in turn makes goal setting feel meaningless.

Expecting instantaneous results and when that does not happen, you conclude that goal setting does not work.

Lack of commitment. You underestimate the efforts and actions that are needed to see a goal be accomplished.

Underdeveloped action plans and an unclear routine to keep you accountable.

Lack of ambition. You prefer to stay in your comfort zone even when it is a miserable course of action, you would still prefer it instead of swimming upstream into unknown waters.

There are plenty of reasons you could use to explain the difficulty of goal setting. This book was written to implore you to use the information to get the outcomes in life that you desire instead of limiting your life's possibilities.

You need to have goals because by setting them, it will help you trigger new behaviors and help you stay focused. Goals also help align your focus and promote a sense of self-mastery. Having goals will help you limit procrastination. Going after what you want in life provides fuel for your journey.

Every season of life comes with its fair share of uncertainty.

When you have goals, you are able to maintain where you are going, because the goals you set provide you with clarity and direction.

Having goals and reaching them promotes confidence in self and provides the fuel and motivation needed to keep challenging yourself to set big goals that will cause you to move out of your comfort zone, forcing you to grow and learn. The more you learn and grow, the more options and possibilities you open yourself up to. Life does not just happen to you. By having goals, you make life happen as you want it to be.

You have three choices in life. You can watch things happen, make things happen, or wonder what will happen.

In order to make things happen in your life, you must write your goals down.

By writing down your goals, it allows you to visually see them. This is important because when you see something, it affects how you act. You are more likely to be productive if you can see what you have to do, instead of just thinking about it.

In an Inc. Magazine newsletter written by Peter Economy, he interviewed Psychology professor Dr. Gail Matthews, at the Dominican University in California. She conducted a study on goal setting with nearly 270 participants. The results? You are 42 percent more likely to achieve your goals if you write them down. Writing your goals down not only forces you to get clear on what, exactly, it is that you want to accomplish, but doing so plays a part in motivating you to complete the tasks necessary for your success. The process of putting your goals on paper will force you to strategize, to ask questions about your current progress, and to brainstorm your plan of attack.

Best-selling author and self-made millionaire Grant Cardone says that he writes his goals down twice a day. Once in the morning and once at night. He explains it like this, "I want to wake up to it. I want to go to sleep to it and I want to dream with it... I want to write my goals down before I go to sleep at night because they are important to me, they are valuable to me, and I get to wake up to them again tomorrow."

Grant was once deep in debt and addicted to drugs. His mother once told him, "The best investment you will ever make is the one you make in yourself." Those words were the fuel he needed to set his goals high and to live life like he wanted. If he can change his life's narrative, so can you. The starting point for all your goals should be envisioning where you want to end up. According to Inc.com columnist, Brent Gleeson, when you envision yourself reaching goals of any kind, your brain starts finding ways to make it happen.

By visualizing yourself hitting a goal, you are actually training your brain to perform in a way that will help you reach that goal. When you visualize yourself hitting a specific goal, your brain interprets that imagery as reality—and creates new neural pathways to support that reality.

In the article, Brent displays the power of envisioning his goals and how he was able to accomplish his goals in life. From his college successes, being a Navy Seal, building a successful fortune 500 business, becoming a motivational speaker, and marrying the women of his dreams, Brent attributes his life successes to having a very detailed mental picture of where he wanted to end up. Brent's advice is to develop a mental picture of what the win looks like and be able to articulate it well. Here is the example that he uses to convey this practice. "If your goal is to compete in a tri-athlon, envision your training regimen. Envision yourself performing during the event. Envision what you want the outcome to be."

For me, my visualization tactics start with a vision board that displays where I want to end up at the end of the goals I set. I use images and not words. With all the creative apps available today, a vision board can be assembled in a short period of time. I display my vision board in various places around my house so that I am constantly seeing where I want to end up. The images get ingrained in my psyche and my thoughts and actions tend to align with the goal that I am pursuing.

Goal setting plays a significant role in how you maneuver in life. Embrace the fact that it is necessary to incorporate goal setting practices into every aspect of your life.

Once you have a goal you want to reach, you now must incorporate a system, or what I refer to as action steps in my book GR8NESS IN THE MAKING, of how you will arrive at your desired outcome. This is what advocates of creating systems are referring to. In my opinion, it's the same thing. You must do something to arrive at your desired outcome.

According to Skill Share, which is an online platform of experts that offer information based on their skills and expertise, advocates for creating systems stress the importance of making sure the system you are incorporating, aligns with the outcomes you want. Here are some of the examples they give:

Goal: losing weight

System: exercising and eating healthy

Goal: getting an A on a test

System: review notes and study daily

The Skill Share site for creating systems emphasizes a three-question process for reaching your destination. (Goal)
1. Set a destination that is your goal
2. Ask questions on how to get there
3. Apply the answer and adjust as needed
They encourage you not to focus totally on the goal, but the system or actions that lead to the goal. I agree with them on the focus element and will add that there must be a Growth Mindset understanding when approaching the goal setting and systems process. No matter where you start, with practice, consistency, and intentional activity toward your targeted outcome, you will eventually arrive at where you want to end up.

None of this is to say that goals are useless. However, I've found that goals are good for planning your progress and systems are good for actually making progress.

Goals can provide direction and even push you forward in the Short-Term, but eventually a well-designed system will always win. Having a system is what matters. Committing to the process is what makes the difference.

In my opinion, there is no great debate whether one should use setting goals or creating systems to achieve and succeed in life. I think it is crucial that both goal setting and creating a system or action steps be incorporated to advance. The key is planning, alignment, and execution.

You should set a big goal and a lot of little goals. This will allow you to celebrate your accomplishment along the way toward your end result.

Goals are good for giving you the incentive to develop your habits or "systems" in the first place. Goals can even spark your imagination when you are struggling for motivation to follow through on daily tasks. Make sure to break your goals down into multiple, manageable steps in order to feel those smaller, daily successes and to not feel overwhelmed by the journey ahead or underwhelmed when you actually accomplish your goal.

The systems approach that advocates like to highlight to replace the goal setting, are simply all the actions you take to achieve your goals. And remember that every goal achieved is the beginning of another goal.

If your goals are hollow, the feeling you get from them will be hollow, but if your goals are meaningful then the sense of accomplishment is meaningful. You have to have Long-Term goals to know what the end result you are seeking is. Create Short-Term goals and apply a system to get you there.

Goals and systems should be used in conjunction to reach your desired life outcomes. Set a goal, then construct a system to get you there and keep in mind that your commitment to your process will determine your progress.

Constructing your life should not be taken lightly. It deserves your time and attention in order for you to truly build and live the life you desire.

Chapter 7
Systems

*Every system is perfectly designed to get
the results it gets"*

- W. Edwards Deming

While researching for this book, I found that there has been much debate as to which one is better: goals or systems?

Over the years, personal development coaches such as Earl Nightingale, Brian Tracy, Jim Rohn, and Zig Ziglar have led millions of people to accomplish and achieve great things in life by stressing the importance of goal setting. Earl Nightingale stressed that you become what you think about because when you set a goal, it becomes your focus and your thoughts and action tend to align with the goal you are seeking. Now there is a new age thought that says setting goals is not necessary. Instead, creating systems to achieve and advance is the secret sauce.

In the book *Atomic Habits*, author James Clear, stresses that goals are good for setting a direction, but systems are best for making progress. He believes that problems arise when you spend too much time thinking about your goals and not enough time designing your systems.

New York Times Best Selling author and Marketing Professor at New York University Stern School of Business, Adam Alter, encourages people not to set goals, but set systems. He feels like goal setting is a broken process. He feels that once you set a goal, you exist in a failure state until you actually reach the goal. He says that goals don't nourish you psychologically and once you reach a goal you really don't get much from it, but a sense of "I need to go find something else because the goal setting leaves an unfulfilled feeling."

Adam encourages systems of habits. He believes the habits that are established will allow the desired outcome to be manifested.

Here is an example of a system according to Adam Alter. If you are writing a book, you do not give any specifics about the book. You approach it by saying, you are writing a book and the system is to sit down every day and write for an hour. Not counting words or evaluating. Just simply sitting down to write. Adam says, you succeed every day as long as you adhere to the system you set. He says every time you stick to a system you are achieving something.

Advocates for systems feel that setting goals are bad because they create anxiety when trying to keep them and when you fail. They feel you go from a high when you're creating a goal and even when you are in pursuit of a goal, to a low when the illusions you've built about your future come crashing against reality.

They believe that when you define a goal, you place limits on yourself, and you create unnecessary stress and pressure. In the article, "Why Goal Setting is Wrong," writer/blogger Debby Germino writes that goal setting can breed a kind of discontentment. For A-type personalities, it becomes an endless stream of striving. As each goal is achieved a new one is set and there is never a moment of satisfaction or ease. It's a constant cycle of one-upping that inevitably leads to burnout. And conversely, when the goal is missed, disappointment sets in leading to discouragement and lack of motivation.

Author James Clear says, "When you're working toward a goal, you are essentially saying, 'I'm not good enough yet, but I will be when I reach my goal.'" Clear feels the problem with this mindset is that you're teaching yourself to always put happiness and success off until the next milestone is achieved. Clear feels that choosing a goal puts a huge burden on your shoulders. He thinks that when you focus on the practice instead of the performance, you can enjoy the present moment and improve at the same time.

Systems advocates want to encourage the building of habits. They believe the habits that are established will allow the desired outcome to be manifested. They believe creating habits is the key because when you develop habits, they extend over into other areas of life after you have succeeded in the daily practice of carrying out the system you set up. They believe that if you do something every day, it is a system as opposed to waiting later to achieve something in the future that's a goal. They feel you should commit to a process and not a goal.

I agree that habits should be honed to make the process of advancement and achievement a way of life. However, I disagree that goal setting should be totally replaced with a systematic approach.

Here's why goals are necessary, as I stated in the previous chapter: Goals are the targets toward which you point your life. Goals give you a starting point and a destination to reach. Goals give you focus and help measure progress. Writing goals down helps you to see where you are going, what changes you need to make, and if you are progressing toward your desired result. So, in essence, the SMART

GOAL approach that I mentioned in the previous chapter, is also a system.

Here's why goals and systems work better together. Everything has a starting point. Your life outcomes start with setting a goal of where you want to end up. Once your goal is set, you then create a way to achieve your goal by incorporating a system or action steps to reach the goal you set. I don't believe one can survive without the other. The elements must coexist in order to build a successful life. Most goals are not achievable without systems, and systems cannot be evaluated without comparing them to the goal they are intended to serve. When you constantly combine the two, achievement, advancement, and elevation in any area of life is possible. You will grow and consistently redefine who you are which in turn creates the habitable practice of becoming a bigger and better you.

The pursuit of your goals will allow you to challenge yourself and grow. The experience is rewarding as it helps you develop into the person you are meant to be.
Goal setting and systems. State the outcome you want then plot the course to accomplish it. Determination and discipline to reach your goal will provide the fuel for your journey.

Chapter 8
Learning Styles/Linear and Non-linear Thinking

"I have a different way of thinking. I think synergistically. I'm not linear in thinking, I'm not very logical"

- IMELDA MARCOS

YOU HAVE JUST READ ABOUT the importance of goal setting and creating systems to help you achieve your goals.

Goal setting and systems are not a one-process-fits-all thing. The way you learn, or your learning style, should be considered in your goal setting and system creation process. Learning style refers to the preferential way in which you absorb, process, comprehend, and retain information.

While receiving information, there are four types of learning styles: visual, auditory, kinesthetic, and reading/writing.

According to educator James Parker, visual learners are the most common type of learner, making up 60 percent of our population. Visual learners relate best to written information, notes, diagrams, and pictures. Visual learners do not work well with someone just telling you information. You work better when you can write the information down.

Parker describes auditory learners as the second most common type of learner, making up almost 30 percent of the population. As an auditory learner, you relate best to the spoken word. You would rather listen to a lecture then take notes afterwards or rely on printed notes. Written information means little to you until you have heard it. It helps when auditory learners read written information aloud.

Parker says kinesthetic learners are a rare breed and make up about 5 percent of the population. Kinesthetic/Tactile learners prefer a hands-on approach. You learn through touch and movement. You learn skills by imitation and practice.

Lastly, there are reading/writing learners that make up about 5 percent of the population. If you are a reading/writing learner, you learn best through words. You prefer to take notes or read in order to learn new information.

In the book, From High School to College, by Dr. Michael W. Kirst, Professor Emeritus of Education and Business Administration at Stanford University, expresses the importance of understanding personal learning styles. Dr. Kirst says it is important to note that everyone has a combination of ways in which they learn; however, most people have ONE predominant learning style. He stresses that no learning style is either better or worse than another. In fact, each learning style has its own strengths and limitations. He advises that if you know your limitations, you can extend your abilities and reach your highest potential. Knowing your learning style is important if you want to achieve to the best of your ability.

Throughout your life, goal setting will be a constant activity. Learning new information to get you to your next level will be ongoing. When you know your learning style and are able to grasp the full understanding of information, it makes the concept of creating a system or action steps to move you toward your goals easier.

You must have the proper information before you can devise your system or plan of action to get you where you are going. Just like there are different learning styles, the same holds true to the way you go about implementing how you will reach your goal.

There are two types of thought processes that you follow when it comes to reaching an end result. It is referred to as linear and non-linear thinking.

Linear thinking is an analytic, methodic, rational, and logical thinking style. A linear process moves forward like a line with a starting point and an ending point, and our brains often want to make simple straight connections in sequential order. On the other hand, non-linear thinking is thoughts that process in multiple directions, rather than in one direction, and based on the concept that there are multiple starting points from which one can apply logic to a problem. In other words, linear thinkers use a step-by-step procedure or method to get them to their end result, whereas non-linear thinkers use an array of methods to get them to the outcome that they desire.

When it comes to creating systems and plans of actions to reach your goals, linear and non-linear thinkers will have to devise their own strategy according to how they think and operate. One is not better or worse than the other. It strictly depends on your individual thinking styles.

While raising my kids, I experienced this firsthand. I have two daughters. My oldest is a linear thinker like I am. Her method of achievement is to follow a step-by-step process and action steps that she creates for herself in order to reach her desired outcomes. On the other hand, my youngest daughter is a non-linear thinker. She is a creative individual. For years, I struggled with guiding her to be as productive as I knew she could be. I was forcing my linear thinking habits and procedures on her non-linear thought processing. I learned to just encourage her to create ways to MOVE FORWARD toward her desired outcomes. I had to resign the reigns to her and allow her to own her own system and action steps that will guide her to reach her desired outcomes.

Author Michael Marshall, believes it is best to have well-balanced skills and thinking in both linear sequential thinking' and non-linear thinking with creativity, innovativeness, and out-of-the-box thinking. He says that both of these thinking abilities and skills are important and needed in every aspect of your life. Even though some individuals may be naturally inclined to one or the other or neither, these are skills that can be learned.

I definitely agree that you should develop both types of learning styles because when you set goals, at some point you will need to incorporate the logical progression which is linear thinking or get creative in how you achieve a goal, which is non-linear thinking. The process of goal setting and system creation will be enhanced when you incorporate both methods of thinking. And just like anything else, the more you practice the process, the better you will get at plotting your approach to reach your goals.

During every season of your life, you will set new goals and face new challenges. How you learn, process, and apply new information will be the determining factor in how you maneuver the various obstacles you will encounter on your journey. Learning is perpetual and an essential part of living your life by design.

Chapter 9
Believe, Develop, Take Action

"Believe in yourself! Have faith in your abilities! Without a humble but reasonable confidence in your own powers you cannot be successful or happy"

- NORMAN VINCENT PEALE

I HAVE A MANTRA THAT I use for myself and in my business that is applicable to the success systems I have created. A mantra is an affirmation to motivate and inspire you to be your best self. It is typically a positive phrase or statement that you use to affirm the way you want to live your life. The four words that I use are Believe, Develop, and Take Action.

Up until this point, you have read about two of the pillars and their components of The Blueprint for Success, Live Life By Design, success system. Great information if I do say so myself; however, it does not matter if it is my success system or somebody else's system. There is one catalyst that will prevent you from implementing any process or procedure that is meant to elevate you. That catalyst is belief in yourself. If you do not believe in yourself and your ability, no system will ever work for you.

Over the years, I'm sure you have heard the phrase, believe in yourself. Or some simply say, be you. Sounds simple enough, yet it becomes a daunting task when you genuinely do not know what that is because you have not been given the information and guidance to help you establish an understanding of who you are as an individual. You only have surface knowledge about your strengths, weaknesses, gifts, talents, hopes, dreams, and vision for your life. These components are talked about at the beginning of this book and are a part of your inner invisible elements that are the true essence of you. These components that are a part of your inner self, are the qualities that allow you to genuinely BE yourself and show up for your life.

It is impossible to believe in something whole-heartedly that you do not know anything about. That is why it is crucial to know the invisible elements that make you who you are. Until you do, you cannot set goals and create systems without trusting that your inner workings will propel you to accomplish anything. Unfortunately for many, the lack of belief in self is where the pursuit of life's grandest desires and possibilities end.

The question then becomes, why is it so difficult for you to believe in yourself? There is an array of reasons that you could use. I say this because I used many of them countless times throughout my life over the years. I have learned that the lack of belief in self is common and a paralyzing experience that is a barrier that keeps you living your life with limits.

Some of the common reasons for lack of belief in self are you grew up hearing negative messages about yourself and your abilities. You fear failure and you focus on past failures. Someone you trusted and respected said something critical about your work or performance. Someone told you that you weren't capable of ever being anything in life. You were told you are too _____. You were told you don't have enough _____. As you can see, there are plenty of reasons to go around. You consistently deny yourself access to truly live when you allow the limiting beliefs you have about yourself to keep you dwelling in a state of mediocrity.

You must stop the negative self-talk and change the story you tell yourself. You must envision where you want to end up and let that be the fuel that ignites you to want to change the trajectory of your life. The system that I have created is progressive. That means you cannot move on to secondary pillars without first doing the foundational work in the first pillar to build on. Remember, this process is about building you. That starts with building your belief in yourself.

Once you embrace your foundational truths and start believing in yourself, it's then time to develop your knowledge, skills, gifts, and talents. As I mentioned before, the road to your best life will involve constantly learning new things that will serve as the bricks to build the life you want. Developing your knowledge and skills will position you for the next stages and challenges that will come during your pursuit to advance yourself.

I choose the word develop as part of my mantra because the word means starting to exist, grow or cause to grow and become more mature, advanced, or elaborate. My process is all about becoming your grandest self and the only way to do that is to continuously develop your knowledge, skills, gifts, and talents at every stage of your journey.

Here's the thing, the way to gain knowledge and information to grow is accessible. With smartphones and a library card that is free, you have access to information and the internet is available twenty-four hours a day. Gone are the days that you are limited to developing yourself due to your lack of finances to afford classes or resources that you need to develop in various areas. My point is that the internet can be your starting point to begin your development. It is my hope that you utilize it as much as possible to gain the knowledge you need to build your skills and advance your gifts and talents.

If you are living your life by continually developing and elevating, at some point you will have to seek specialized information and training. At this point, you will be opening doors of opportunity that will only be accessible to those of you who have put in the work to advance. This is a great sign and means that you are on track to becoming the best version of yourself and living the life you desire.

Now, after you have established your foundation and developed yourself, it is time to take action. Taking action simply means to diligently do the things that are going to help you reach the goals you are on your quest to reach. Your thoughts and action should be deliberate and should align with your vision of where you want to end up. Taking action ensures that the outcomes you seek will be manifested because your actions and systems are intentional toward your desired outcomes.

So, on your life's journey and in the pursuit to live your life by design, remember to BELIEVE in yourself, DEVELOP your knowledge, skills, gifts, and talents, and TAKE ACTION to achieve your goals, hopes, and dreams.

We have come to the final pillar of The Blueprint for Success process. The whole concept has been about designing, constructing, and now maintaining the life that you want to live. I will recap what we have discussed so far.

The theme has been the correlation between building a house and building a life. The process begins with the Design Pillar. Whenever something is being built, it all starts with planning out the specific foundational elements that are essential for the desired results. When designing a life, it must be founded on the personalized vision, hopes, dreams, attributes, and mindset of the individual.

The second pillar of the process is the Construction Pillar. Goals, systems, and action steps are vital to The Blueprint For Success process. These components, when practiced and mastered, will lead one to achieve the results and outcomes that are desired. Intentional activity toward the desired outcome is key.

Now, we have arrived at the final pillar of The Blueprint For Success process. I refer to it as the Maintenance Pillar. The upkeep on any house must be done on a continuous basis. Things must be repaired, replaced, or upgraded to remain functional. The same holds true for the life of the individual that seeks to live it successfully. The main purpose of regular maintenance is to ensure that all pillars of the Blueprint process are operating at 100 percent efficiency at all times.

The correlation of repair, replace, and upgrade translates into elevation and constant revisions of mindset, goals, and systems for an individual. The consistency to always become the best version of self, and to reach the greatness potential that lives in every human being, is the plight for the person that seeks to live a successful life.

Success at any level requires discipline and commitment which forces the individual to constantly challenge himself. This phenomenon is called moving outside your comfort zone. When that is done, it helps the individual create new normals, which become the measure and standard for being able to overcome obstacles and still accomplish and achieve.

Chapter 10
The Great 8 Formula

"When you are not willing to be challenged, disturbed, or offended, you are not willing to explore your weaknesses or ever reach your highest potential."

- BRYANT McGILL

As I MENTIONED BEFORE, I am passionate about creating systems and formulas. This book is actually the second success system that I have created. The first system was created in 2018 and published in my book titled, *GR8NESS IN THE MAKING*. It is what I call the Great 8 Formula.

I must share with you how the formula came about. Most of my life I felt totally invisible, helpless, and like I was imprisoned with no way to escape. As a four-year-old, I felt like a death sentence was placed on my life. I was repeatedly told that I was dumb and because of the negative words of others, my sense of self was bound, handcuffed, shackled, and left for dead. I had concluded that I was incapable of learning and therefore not worthy to be loved. The prison of pain eventually turned to me mastering the art of being invisible in my daily dealing. Separating my inner self from my physical self was my way of coping and maneuvering in life.

At the age of nineteen, I found myself in prison yet again and feeling helpless because of the boy that displayed his misguided love for me with the words and deeds that were mentally, emotionally, and physically abusive. The constant threat to end my life as well as the life of my family members kept me living in a prison of fear for six years. Then, in 2003 after the birth of my second daughter I was diagnosed with a severe case of postpartum depression which felt like a prison all over again.

I often wondered why I had to endure such pain and how much more I could take? It was at that point that I looked at my two daughters and decided that I didn't want them to live a life with limits like I had. I decided that I was going to do everything I could to bring out the greater person that was inside of me. So I started to rebuild myself internally. I had to establish what vision I wanted for my life as well as my hopes, dreams, gifts, talents, and attributes. The more I learned and accomplished, the more confident I felt in my ability to excel at anything. For the first time in my life, living life without limits was possible.

While on my journey of self-discovery, there were a lot of obstacles, challenges, learning curves, failed attempts, and uncertainty, but everything I experienced was necessary to bring out the greater person that lived within me. I had to get out of my comfort zone which forced me to encounter a lot of struggles. But I learned to view struggle as a growing process, and I started embracing challenges because they helped me elevate to my new normals.

While in search of self, I often heard the phrase, "You have greatness inside of you." Every motivational speaker used this phrase. I believed the phrase whole-heartedly; however, I discovered that there had never been an actual step-by-step procedure or formula that could be implemented to actually get me to my greatness potential.

I remember it like it was yesterday. I had worked sixteen hours at my then job in the airline industry. I was exhausted to say the least, but I had promised myself that I was going to be a good role model for my daughters and that included me building my own personal development business. I sat at the kitchen table and began to adjust my personal logo which at the time was a capital R with a key lock on it. Underneath the R, I wrote these words, "Unlock the greatness within, you are greatness in the making." It was like a lightning bolt hit me in the head. Almost instantaneously, the Great 8 Formula was born. I began to run around the house reciting the formula that had been given to me. That was on June 21, 2017. Ten months later the book GR8NESS IN THE MAKING was published.

When GR8NESS IN THE MAKING was being written, I had no idea that it was a piece to an even bigger puzzle of helping you create your own personalized blueprint for success so that you can live your life by design.

Going back to the theme of a house being designed, constructed, and then maintained, again that same concept applies to your life if you want to be successful. In essence, the Great 8 Formula serves as the maintenance pillar for the Blueprint for success system. In other words, it's a standalone system as well a part of another system.

The word GREATNESS is the basis for the formula. It encompasses eight critical elements that must be applied so that the potential for greatness will manifest in your life.

The Great 8 Formula is as follows:
Goals
Resilience
Effort
Attitude
Teachable/Trainable
Navigate
Execute
Standards
Success

This formula is a self-accountability tool that can be used to help you maintain and elevate in every season of your life. So here are the eight elements again with an explanation. This is only a short variation of the formula, but I would encourage you to get the book, GR8NESS IN THE MAKING, for a more in-depth version that I believe will help you in your life.

When these eight elements are applied during the various situations, circumstances, obstacles, or challenges that are sure to come in life, success emerges for that particular part of the journey, due to the application of the formula.

It has been my experience and the experience of my clients and focus groups that were polled while crafting the Great 8 Formula, that if there was a formula to apply to life, it would have saved them from a lot of mistakes as a result of the lack of knowledge, information, and experience.

This formula is a self-accountability tool that can be used to help maintain and elevate the individual. So here are the eight elements again with an explanation. This is only a short variation of the formula, but I would encourage you to get the book, GR8NESS IN THE MAKING, for a more in-depth version that I believe will help you on your life's journey. By providing this guide that aids with sequential achievement and accomplishment, the formula ushers in elevated thoughts and actions that can be maintained for future seasons of life.

The Great 8 Formula is as follows:

Goals

I covered goals and its role in the Construction Pillar; however, its importance deserves to be repeated. Goal is a specific objective that you want to achieve in the future. Without a goal, advancement and elevation in life is impossible. Goals are the targets toward which you point your life. Goals give you a starting point and a destination to reach. Goals give you focus and help measure progress. Writing goals down helps you to see where you are going, what changes you need to make, and if you are progressing toward your desired result.

Resilience

The ability to adapt to change. To exercise resilience, some change or circumstance has to take place. During the process of achievement and elevating in life, the boundaries of your comfort zone will be challenged.

As mentioned in the Design Pillar, this is when the subconscious mindset is at its peak.

It has memorized all your comfort zones and it works to keep you in them. Your subconscious mind causes you to feel emotionally and physically uncomfortable whenever you attempt to do anything new or different. It goes against changing any of your established patterns of behavior. Resilience must be exhibited to reach new normals and your potential for greatness.

Life is filled with uncertainties. The only thing that is certain in life is the fact that the element of change is sure to affect every aspect of your life, time and time again. Changes that affect your life will come in the form of setbacks, heartache, heartbreak, let downs, disappointment, mishaps, mis-steps, challenges, circumstances, and obstacles.

You exercise resilience when the winds of life force you to

recreate, reinvent, or reposition yourself. Your ability to adapt and overcome allows you to build your resilience gene.

Sometimes it will feel like life has gotten the best of you. It is during those times when that thing that lies deep within forces you to muster up enough strength to bounce back after life has dealt a blow that was so severe it would cause you to give up on life. The resilience gene should help you cope with your season of unrest. It should sustain you while you recover from the changes that occur.

Effort

There must be relentless effort toward reaching goals, hopes, and dreams. The best plans are useless if there is no effort or action taken to reach the desired outcome. By putting in the effort, you know what you are capable of. When you make an effort, it teaches you that you can do more than you thought. You learn new skills and abilities when you take the time to put in consistent effort.

One of my mentors, Celebrity Mindset Consultant Stan Pearson II, says it like this, "Effort on fire beats knowledge on ice." That simply means that when you truly put forth the effort to do something, you will win over the person that just has the knowledge.

Rory Vaden, author of *Take the Stairs: 7 Steps for Achieving True Success*, says "What you do today, the effort you put in, determines your success tomorrow." In a blog post from *Strength for Life*, the writer of the "Power of Effort" post says, "Every new success that you achieve through your efforts increases your confidence in yourself and your abilities. Effort keeps you focused on success."

When I say effort, I don't mean simply going through the motions. Your results, or lack thereof, will be an indicator as to how much effort you really exert. Your continuous effort is required when you are living your life by design.

Attitude

Attitude is everything. It affects the way you feel about yourself or certain situations or circumstances that you will find yourself in. Attitude check is crucial especially when you are trying to elevate and constantly be the best version of yourself. There will be a lot of uncomfortable situations and times of struggle, but strength is gained during these times and a positive attitude will help during the process.

Your attitude is what influences all your actions. It is only the right attitude, which gets you good results. You must embody a never-give-up attitude in order to view your mistakes, missteps, and failures as an opportunity to try it again a different way or with a different focus. Maintaining a positive attitude on your journey is key.

Teachable/Trainable

Being teachable means you are willing to change so you can transform and excel. With this mindset you understand that you do not have all the answers. It is crucial for you to surround yourself with others that have the wisdom, knowledge, and experience to get you where you are trying to go.

Being teachable is going to make you feel vulnerable and uncomfortable, but it is necessary in order to elevate you to your next level. Your inability to learn from others will derail your progress and keep you from realizing your vision, hopes, and dreams.

You must be able to use feedback, either positive or critical, as a way to improve. You should take advantage of every opportunity to keep getting better at your skills.

Navigate

Life's journey can be viewed as taking a trip in a car. On the road you will encounter roadblocks, detours, and non-accessible avenues. It is then when you must use your internal navigational tool to recalculate where you are in reference to where you want to go. Reevaluate the desired outcome and redo the system or action steps to get there. The way you respond to life or what happens in life is key to being able to back up and regroup so you can restart your journey.

Execute

The definition of execute is the carrying out or putting into effect a plan, order, or a course of action. Before you can execute, you must have a plan. It is great to have a plan in place that will give you a layout or Blueprint on what needs to be done to get the finished product or desired result. It does not matter if you have a plan in place, failure to take any action steps or implement a system, you will not reach your desired outcome.

Execution requires constantly aligning your actions with the results you desire to see.

Standards

In order to set yourself apart, you must continuously raise your standards. People should know you by your work ethic and the standards you set. Standards are something you live, breath, and try to get to no matter what. Whenever an obstacle or situation threatens to interrupt or sabotage your plans, your above and beyond approach to the challenges in life will help meet and exceed personal standards. Only the GREAT live by a standard that is unlike much of the population. Raising your standards will be a lasting change element on your road to greatness. Changing for the better, mastering new skills, gaining new knowledge, and conquering obstacles is a way of life when you continuously try to better your best and reach your greatness potential.

The final S in the word GREATNESS is the result of accomplishing SUCCESS. In the Maintenance Pillar, when the Great 8 Formula is applied, success is sure to follow during every season of life.

So what I've created is a formula that allows you to identify which element you need to apply to any given situation or goal you are pursuing.

Here's an example of how to identify and apply the elements of the formula.

A little over a year ago, my daughter came home from school several days in a row complaining about one of her classes. She can generally police herself by using the Great 8 Formula, but for some reason, she couldn't get past her ill feelings about this particular class. I finally began to walk her through the formula application to help her determine where she was.

Here is the dialog:

Me: What is the **goal** you are seeking?

Response: To get an A in the class.

Me: Are you writing a paper and it's making you feel overwhelmed, and you are needing to exercise **resilience** to get through it?

Response: No, I turned in my paper last week.

Me: Are you learning something that is difficult, and you need some **tutoring**?

Response: No, I know all the material, I've turned in all my work. I currently have an A.

It was at that point that she blurted out, "It's my **attitude.**" She recognized that she had gotten annoyed with a few of her classmates, and she had been dreading having any encounters with them. She made a mental note to herself to resolve the issue with them the next day.

As you maneuver through your journey, with every new goal you will experience each of the elements in the formula. Having a formula to actually apply to where you are is the key.

Think about it:

You set a **goal.**

When things get challenging, you don't quit, you exercise **resilience** to maintain you where you are so that you can learn new knowledge or build new skills.

You make the **effort** to do the things you need to do to move you toward your desired result.

Check your **attitude** regularly. Only a positive attitude will benefit you.

Do you need to be **taught** something? Be willing to learn from others.

Is the plan of action or system you set in need of redirecting or **navigating**? Sometimes you have to back up and go in a different direction.

Are you **executing** the action steps or systems to reach your desired outcome?

Do you need to raise your **standards** to get your desired results?

By applying this formula, you practice self-accountability. The maintenance mechanism of checking and reflecting on where you were before, where you are now, and where you are wanting to go.

This process is perpetual and can be applied to every aspect of your life.

Chapter 11
The Great 8 Formula in Action

"Greatness is not a destination, it is a continuous journey that never ends"

- AUTHOR UNKNOWN

WHEN I FIRST CREATED THE Great 8 Formula, I started researching successful people and discovered that in some way, shape, or form successful people practice the elements in the formula. Take tennis superstar Serena Williams for example. Serena grew up in poverty-stricken Compton, California. She started playing tennis at the age of four. The likeliness of her being a tennis professional was unachievable to most people. But, in an interview at the age of eight, when asked what she wanted to be when she grew up, Serena replied, "A tennis star and to win the US Open." I'm sure a lot of people discarded her vision and her dream of becoming a tennis star. The odds of a poor black girl from Compton, California that hardly had a decent tennis court to practice on, becoming a tennis professional, let alone a tennis superstar, was impossible in the eyes of the tennis world.

Serena did not let any of the naysayers deter her. Her family sacrificed a lot to allow her to train and hone her skills that would make her unstoppable on the court when she arrived on the tennis circuit at age fourteen. From 1995 to 1999, Serena played on the professional circuit, defeating many of the top ranked players at the time. In 1999, Serena would achieve her goal of winning the U.S. Open, by defeating number one ranked Martina Hingis. That was the beginning of an era.

To date, Sarena has won twenty-three Grand Slam singles titles, fourteen Grand Slam doubles titles with her sister, and two other Grand Slam mixed doubles titles. She is considered by most to be the Greatest Of All Time in women's tennis. Not only has Serena influenced the world of athletics, but she has also influenced the community, specifically girls and women of color. But Serena did not just stop there, she had other dreams for her life. Serena is also an entrepreneur and has a fashion line and is part owner of a professional football team. According to Celebrity Net Worth, Serena Williams is worth $200 million. From her on the court earnings, corporate endorsements, and her entrepreneur endeavors, Serena Williams is living her life by design.

I mentioned Serena because not only did she design her life with her vision, hopes, dreams, strengths, weakness, and attributes, she constructed it with her goals and systems that allowed her to achieve her desired outcomes. Her continued elevation throughout her tennis career and for her business ventures, required her to continuously set **goals**, be **resilient** when times were hard, always make an **effort** to get better, have a positive **attitude**, follow the **teachings** of her coaches, **navigate** the path to reach her desired outcomes, **execute** every plan put in place, and constantly raise the **standards** for herself and became **successful**. She repeatedly reached her potential for greatness. A glimpse into the life of Serena Williams provides an illustration of how the Great 8 Formula can look for you when you apply it to your life daily.

Another person that exhibits the Great 8 Formula in action, is none other than actor, producer, and philanthropist, Tyler Perry.

Tyler Perry grew up in an abusive home as a child. A lot of his childhood memories are not particularly good ones. His father abused his mother and him constantly inside the home. Outside the home ,Tyler was taken advantage of by both men and women. His childhood was so bad that he changed his name from Emmitt Perry Jr., which was his father's name as well, to Tyler Perry just to distance himself from the man that left outer and inner scars from his abusive tactics.

For many years, Tyler was angry and confused about a lot of things he experienced. In 1991, he was watching Oprah Winfrey on her talk show, and he heard her say that writing things down could be cathartic. Tyler began writing letters to himself in a journal, which became his first script for the play, I Know I've Been Changed. This first script was the beginning of Tyler's career in the entertainment business.

To fund his first play, Tyler used his life savings of $12,000. His goal was to help others that may have experienced some of the challenges and trauma that he displayed in his play. Unfortunately, only thirty people showed up on opening night. From 1992-1998, every show that Tyler put on failed. Tyler believed in himself and was so passionate about the impact he would make on the lives of others, that he would find ways to fund the production by working odd jobs and when he could not pay his rent, he would live in his car or in homeless shelters. His mother begged him to get a steady job, but Tyler would not give up on his dream of being in the entertainment business.

In 2005, Tyler's dream came to fruition when he partnered with Lionsgate Studio to produce and act in the movie, *Diary of a Mad Black Woman*. He has partnered with the studio for several other movies and has ticket sales of over a billion dollars.

Tyler Perry is incredibly talented, but he was dismissed by many people in Hollywood and the entertainment industry. Because of all the rejection he received, in 2008 Tyler decided to open his own movie studio in Atlanta, Georgia. The studio is housed on over 330 acres. Because Tyler's entertainment business grew, he was able to employ many people in the Atlanta area. As of this book's writing, according to Forbes, Perry is said to be worth $1 billion.

Tyler Perry is truly an example of living out the Great 8 Formula. Time and time again he set **goals,** exercised **resilience** when times were hard and uncertain**,** he made an **effort** regardless of the many obstacles they tried to deter him**,** he had the positive **attitude** to keep moving toward his dream, he was able to learn and be **taugh**t by others**,** he had to **navigate** the various paths that his journey took him on. Detouring whenever he needed and finding the paths that would lead him to his intended destinations, he **executed** every plan that would enable him to continue to elevate himself personally and professionally, and he constantly had to raise his **standards** to be a better version of himself during every season of his life. By combining these attributes continuously, Tyler was able to become **successful.** Another illustration of the Great 8 Formula in action.

Once I crafted the formula, I began to examine successful people's life's journeys. It did not take me long to see that the elements in the formula were exhibited consistently. I remember that moment as if it were yesterday. I realized the formula to greatness had been hidden in plain sight. Exhibited daily by many, but never presented as a viable process to achieve the greatness status. Inside I was jumping up and down as if I had won the lottery. I felt like David slaying the giant of separation, inferiority, and lack. I thought to myself, finally there is a way to conceptualize this thing called GREATNESS. I thought, finally there is a way to apply and measure yourself according to a formula that can keep you focused and guide you to reach your potential for greatness in every aspect of your life as well as during every season of your life. I thought, no longer will greatness be a non-attainable phenomenon that only a select few feel like they are worthy of attaining, but a trend that would be a common practice in society. That day, I vowed to impact the masses by introducing them to The Great 8 Formula. It is my desire that greatness become the norm to many and not the exception for a few.

As mentioned before, when I wrote the book GR8NESS IN THE MAKING, which includes this formula, I had no idea it would be a part of a larger piece to the puzzle of personal growth, advancement, and achievement. In my continued search for my own elevation, I learned there are other elements that are also crucial to living a successful life. By combining them with the Great 8 Formula, I was able to create the success system that you have read about in this book.

As a recap, there are three pillars to The Blueprint For Success system.

Pillar One is all about making sure you develop the invisible elements of yourself because that is the foundation you will be using to build your life on. Secondly, Pillar Two is the construction of your life. This is about knowing where you want your life to go and constructing the goals and systems that will lead you there. Lastly, Pillar Three, maintenance. Once you climb or elevate throughout the various stages of your life, you will need to use a maintenance regime, i.e. the Great 8 Formula, that will help you stabilize your position before continuing on to your next season of life. The three pillars are a guide to help you strategically plan, execute, and live the life you want.

Conclusion

You have just been introduced to The Blueprint For Success, Live Life By Design process.

I started this book in October 2020. The day I completed the first draft was on January 6, 2021. I mention this day because on that day there was an attempted coup to take over the government of the United States. The current president, Donald Trump, incited a riot because of the election he lost in November of 2020. I mentioned this at the beginning of the book and the significance of this is that it was white privilege people who started this country, enslaved blacks, and kept them ignorant. In 2021, the same mindsets still run rampant in America. It is really a bad time right now because the whole world is watching, and the United States is supposed to be civilized and superior. This all goes back to the reason why this book was so important for me to write. People of color or people who have been on the other side of the coin of the achievement and wealth gap, now have a way to elevate themselves and design their life the way they see fit. The information in this book will set you apart and provide you an edge that will produce a variety of life options for you to pursue.

Writing this book was a Blueprint experience for me. There were a number of challenges, to say the least. It seemed like I was being deterred on all fronts from completing the book, but because I embody many of the traits that I talk about in this book, I was still able to write and research while working two jobs to keep my family going and continuing to move forward in my life's journey.

Motivational Speaker Les Brown says, "You have to be hungry to go after the life you want." I echo Les Brown's philosophy of being hungry and embrace that I am hungry for change. I am hungry to see the achievement and wealth gap disappear. I am hungry to see people do the work of embodying the mindset and understanding what it takes to design, construct, and maintain a successful life.

In closing, I would like to encourage you to:

Believe in yourself and your ability
Learn something every day
Understand you are capable of being successful
Enjoy the journey
Persistence when challenges and obstacles come
Be **Relentless** and stay focused on your goals
Have **Integrity**, be honest never compromise yourself
Navigate the noise that is sure to come to deter your efforts
Trust the process that will lead you to success

You have been given a Blueprint to follow. Go, Live Your Life By Design.

Acknowledgements

I WOULD LIKE TO ACKNOWLEDGE the people who have stood by me, encouraged me, and pushed me when I didn't have a clue as to what I needed to do next. While birthing this project, life was happening to me, attempting to derail my efforts of producing information that would positively impact the masses. It was the words and actions of others that forced me to stay focused and stay the course to complete this book.

To my husband, Charles, and daughters, Carrington and Cara, thank you for letting me be me and obliging me when I invaded your space to work and infringed on your time when I needed to voice my thoughts. To my mother, Elaine, thank you for your prayers, encouragement, and unconditional love. You often reference me as your Eagle and tell me to fly higher and higher. Many days those words were the only thing that kept me going. To my spiritual advisor and brother, Rodney Jr., thank you for your prayers and guidance and for continuously reminding me of who I was called to be.

To my mentors, Odell and Stan, you met me where I was and provided guidance and support that allowed me to move into the arena of student success and speaking. You are a dynamic duo. To my accountability partners, Staci and Kisha, you pulled me to places that I did not know existed. You added to me on so many levels and in so many ways. Being in my life during this time was not a coincidence, but divinely orchestrated. Thank you for sharing your gifts with me. To Linda and Renee, thank you for your prayers and your GIF text. They were always right on time. To Amy who volunteered her studio and her time to take the cover photos for this book, thank you. To Katie for your graphic creations that depicted the true essence of how this book is aimed to impact.

To my family and friends who served as my focus groups, encouraged me with your words, or provided resources of your gifts and talents, this project would not be complete without you. Because of you, and there are many, I will acknowledge you by first names: Uncle Ricky, Rolanda W., Robin W., Ronica B., Rodria G., Ramon W., Rushawnda W., Tracy W., Sharmien W., Eschell G., Rico W., Raekeisha W., Shonta J., Kevin W. Jr., Raven W., Raielle W., Railyn W., Rodney W. III, Jada J., Zonia R., Robin Ho., Stephanie B., Patrice Y., Virilyah S., Erin B., Chris M., Jamal W., Charles M., Tanya M., Paulita B., Derrick Y.' Robin Hi., Deadrick G., Tia E., Eve M., D'Anna G., Ninja M., John V., and Ava C.

Lastly, to my editor Geo, thank you for your encouraging emails and words of wisdom. You gave me comfort that allowed me to move forward to complete this book.

About The Author

Ramona Rogers has been an entrepreneur for over twenty years. Ramona has captured a way to communicate how she was able to transform the once held belief that she was destined for less than greatness. Her early years of being negatively labeled caused her to have a fixed mindset, and she thought it was legitimate. For it was doctors, teachers, and even loved ones that placed those labels on her. They didn't understand the power of their beliefs, or quite frankly, their misinterpretations of a child who did not yet have the words, tools, environment, or experience to show them just how erroneous their assessments were.

Those early experiences left her feeling inadequate and caused her to develop limiting beliefs about who she was and her possibilities in life.

She experienced a lack of self-confidence for many years, but it wasn't until after she became a mother and experienced a severe case of postpartum depression that her will to live life differently, so that she could be an example for her daughters, became her new outlook on life. In an effort to build herself internally, she began to recognize her ability to relate to people, and to be well received by others. Slowly, she started applying these efforts to academia, an area she once believed she was not destined to shine in. But shine she does! Three books, two curriculums, and various successful business ventures later, she has decided to convert her strategy into a tangible product to share with the rest of the world.

Ramona is the CEO of Ramona Rogers Enterprises. She created the company because she believes that everyone should have an opportunity to live life without limits. By creating personal development educational tools and resources, individuals can continuously become the best possible version of themself. Ramona believes that achievement and advancement should be the norm and not the exception.

Call To Action

You were born to be great and live life to the fullest. I would love to help you create your Blueprint for Success so that you can live your life by design. Go to ramonarogers.com to sign up for my coaching services and mastermind courses. Your best life awaits you.

Follow me on social media:

Facebook: Ramona Rogers

Instagram: ramona_rogers_

LinkedIn: Ramona Rogers

Made in the USA
Middletown, DE
21 September 2021